This Book Belongs To

____

For Anna, Mia, and Mateo

First Edition: March 3, 2026

ISBN: 978-1-0693991-8-2

This book was typeset in Nunito

Written and Designed by Adrian Wise
Illustrated by Alef Ikeda

AdrianWiseBooks@gmail.com
Instagram: @TheAdrianWise

Small
but Mighty
Lifty's Big Day
Farmer Matty's Pasture
Construction Site
barn
Adrian Wise

The sun peeked over Farmer Matty's fields.

This was the day everyone had been waiting for.

"Today's the big day!" beeped Little Lifty, bouncing on his tires.

"We're helping Farmer Matty build a pasture for his new animal friends!"

Lifty couldn't wait.
Not even for one more second.

Lifty rolled over the hill and gasped.
"Oh wow... the whole town is here!"

In the parking lot, side by side,
stood the biggest, strongest machines
Lifty had ever seen.

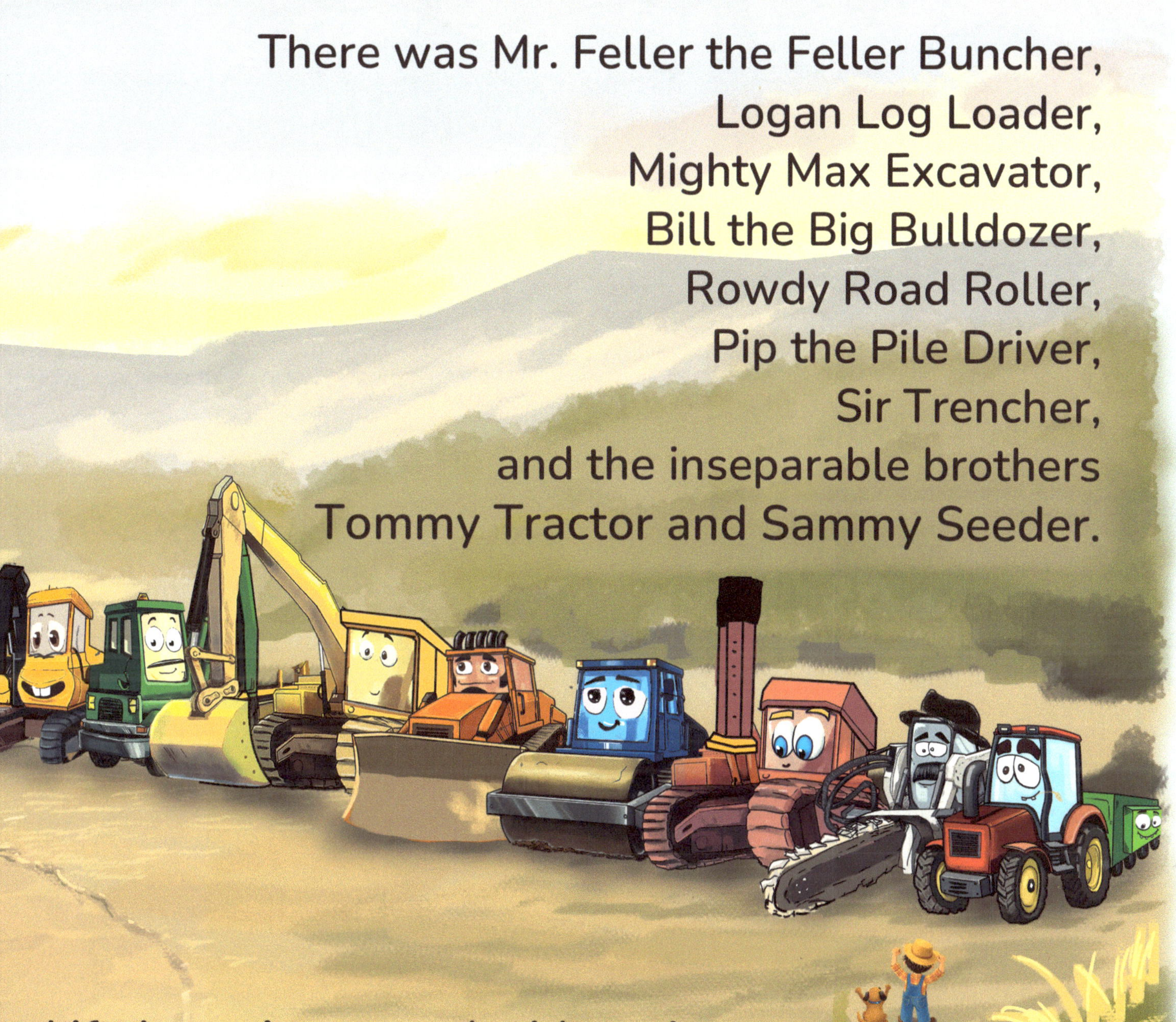

There was Mr. Feller the Feller Buncher,
Logan Log Loader,
Mighty Max Excavator,
Bill the Big Bulldozer,
Rowdy Road Roller,
Pip the Pile Driver,
Sir Trencher,
and the inseparable brothers
Tommy Tractor and Sammy Seeder.

Lifty's engine purred with excitement,
ready to find out who needed his help first.

So Lifty rolled up to Mr. Feller the Feller Buncher, *beep-beep! Vroom-vroom!*

"Hi Mr. Feller! How can I help?"

Mr. Feller chuckled.
"I'm cutting down big trees to make space for the pasture.
I've got giant saw arms for gripping and slicing trunks."

Lifty looked at his **little forks**.
"I don't have saw arms…"

"That's alright," Mr. Feller said kindly.
"Why don't you see if Logan Log Loader needs help?"

BUZZZ!

So Lifty rolled up to Logan Log Loader,
beep-beep, vroom-vroom!

"Hi Logan! How can I help?"

Logan smiled.
"I'm a log truck and loader all in one! I've
got a long hydraulic arm with a big claw
that grabs the heavy logs. Mr. Feller cuts
them down, and I stack them right here
on my own flatbed."

Lifty looked at his **little forks.**
"I don't have a big claw…"

"That's alright," Logan said kindly. "Why
don't you see if Mighty Max Excavator
needs help?"

So Lifty rolled up to Mighty Max Excavator,
beep-beep, vroom-vroom!

"Hi Max! How can I help?"

Mighty Max grinned.
"I'm digging a pond so the animals have
water to drink.
I've got a long arm and a big bucket for
scooping dirt."

Lifty looked at his **little forks**.
"I don't have a big bucket..."

"That's alright,"
Max said kindly.
"Why don't you see if Bill the Big Bulldozer
needs help?"

So Lifty rolled up to Bill the Big Bulldozer, *beep-beep, vroom-vroom!*

"Hi Bill! How can I help?"

Bill roared proudly.
"I'm pushing the dirt Max digs up. I've got a wide, strong blade for shoving huge piles."

Lifty looked at his **little forks.**
"I don't have a big blade..."

"That's alright,"
Bill said kindly.
"Why don't you see if Rowdy Road Roller needs help?"

PUSH!

So Lifty rolled up to Rowdy Road Roller,
beep-beep, vroom-vroom!

"Hi Rowdy! How can I help?"

Rowdy rumbled.
"I'm flattening the ground after Bill pushes
it. I've got a heavy drum to press it
smooth."

Lifty looked at his **little forks.**
"I don't have a heavy drum…"

"That's alright,"
Rowdy said kindly.
"Why don't you see if Pip the Pile Driver
needs help?"

SMOOSH!

So Lifty rolled up to Pip the Pile Driver,
beep-beep, vroom-vroom!

"Hi Pip! How can I help?"

Pip hammered down with a mighty clang.
"I'm pounding posts into the ground for the
fence. I've got a big hammer head that
drives them deep."

Lifty looked at his **little forks.**
"I don't have a hammer head..."

"That's alright,"
Pip said kindly.
"Why don't you see if Sir Trencher needs
help?"

BAM!

So Lifty rolled up to Sir Trencher, beep-beep, vroom-vroom!

"Hi Sir Trencher! How can I help?"

Sir Trencher bowed.
"I'm digging a trench from the river to the pond so the water can flow in. I've got a strong digging chain that chews right through dirt."

Lifty looked at his **little forks**.
"I don't have a digging chain…"

"That's alright," Sir Trencher said kindly.
"Why don't you see if Tommy Tractor and Sammy Seeder need help?"

So Lifty rolled up to Tommy Tractor and
Sammy Seeder,
beep-beep, vroom-vroom!

"Hi Tommy! Hi Sammy! How can I help?"

Tommy chuckled. "We're planting grass
seeds for the pasture."
Sammy added, "I've got a seeder that
sprinkles the seeds behind me."

Lifty looked at his little forks.
"I don't have a seeder..."

"That's alright," Sammy said kindly.
"Thank you for offering, Lifty. I'm sure
there's something you can do."

Lifty's tires drooped. He rolled to the side,
feeling smaller than ever.

Just then, a loud horn honked.

A big delivery truck rumbled in, pulling a long flatbed trailer stacked with heavy wooden crates.

Inside… were Farmer Matty's new animals!

"Oh no!"

Farmer Matty gasped.

"The crates are heavy, and the trailer bed is too high. None of the big machines have the right attachments to grab them!

What should we do now?"

What should
we do now?

So Lifty rolled up to the trailer,
beep-beep, vroom-vroom!

"I can do it! I can help!"

He zoomed to the trailer, raised his forks
up high, slid them under the first crate,
lifted gently, and carried it to the pasture
gate.

One by one, he brought the rest of the
crates until all the animals were reunited in
their new cozy home.

The cows mooed, the pigs oinked, and the
turkeys gobble-gobbled as they peeked
out of their boxes, ready for their new life.

Beep beep, vroom vroom!

All the big machines cheered from
the edge of the pasture.

"Small but mighty, that's our Lifty!"
roared Bill the Bulldozer.

Farmer Matty patted Lifty's hood.
"You brought my new friends home safe.
We couldn't have done it without you."

The animals settled into their new pasture,
safe and snug at last.

Lifty beamed.

"I may not be good at everything…
but we're all good at something."

Later that evening,
with mud on his tires and dust on his forks,
Lifty rolled into the barn feeling mighty.

A GOAT ON A BOAT
Perfect for ages 3-6
Rhyming Bedtime Adventure
ADRIAN
ADVENTURE
For Curious Little Explorers

TO THE MOON, MR. RACCOON
Perfect for Ages 3-5
Bedtime Favorite
ADRIAN
IMAGINATION
For Big Dreamers

RAINY DAY RESCUE
COURAGE IN THE RAIN
WISE
COURAGE
For Brave Little Hearts

Buzz, Moo, Hop!
The Farm That Rhymed
DISCOVERY
Learning Through Rhyme